Metro Mona Lisa

by Rick Leddy

Metro Mona Lisa

ISBN-13: 978-0692378618
ISBN-10: 0692378618

Cover art by Rick Leddy
Edited by Rick Leddy
Book design by Rick Leddy

www.metromonalisa.com

Give feedback on the book at:
metromonalisa@gmail.com

Twitter: @metromonalisa

First Edition

Printed in the U.S.A

To the thousands of people who take the L.A. Metro each day:
No, I don't have any spare change.

Libido Falling
Falling
Libido Falling
Libido Falling

Art student

On the Red Line Train

Stands next to her Neon Green Beach Cruiser

A short polka dot skirt

And long, thin legs

Blackened by sheer tights

A Hello Kitty tattoo

Peers tantalizingly above a low-cut black blouse

Her inviting azure eyes unreflected

behind large neon unlensed frames

And all I can ask is

Why?

Why choose such a heavy bicycle

to tramp up station steps?

My Libido increasingly

Trumped by Practicality

It Smells

I am going to meet Vanora at her work
Near 9th and Broadway
by the Orpheum
near the new Urban Outfitters.
It is either a brave or stupid move.
I walk from 5th to 9th down Broadway
It is late and shadows rustle
The dark shapes on Broadway
swallowing the losing light
are not hip to the Downtown Renaissance
and The Promise of A Golden Future
of sweatered walking dogs and brightly lit cafes;
They sleep on sweating sidewalks
covered in plastic bags and fetid air
Fused heaps of humanity and refuse.
An unoccupied wheelchair like a sculpture
Is parked in front of dark building entrance
Why?
Old reflexes spring to life
I walk fast Anticipating.
Lizard brain mapping escape routes
Fight or Flight
Finally. I am there.
Ubiquitous film crew is shooting...
Something. Again. At the restaurant next door.
Crew stands awaiting Alpha dog
while a woman insistently
Snaps and barks Hollywood Importance

I tuck into the building
And take the elevator to the 6th Floor and
Vanora peers out from the entrance.
She looks tired and worn
and She says to me
It Smells Like Rain.
I shrug.
Only clear skies Downtown tonight
With a 100 percent Chance of Despair.
She works to weave fashionista dreams
until finally, we leave.
At the exit door in the lobby
We look outside.
And it is raining
In sheets
A torrent of droplets slamming and reflecting
neon light dancing against flat concrete stage.
It is Raining in Los Angeles
But it is a false promise
As a slick automobile drives up
Cut!
Just more illusory Hollywood salvation;
a temporary reprieve from dry destiny.
We wait inside
until a worker shuts down the downpour
Our feet splash in twenty feet
of wet and shiny as we leave.
And it smells like rain

Like Rain

Rick Leddy

Saul of L.A.

Saw God Today
At 3rd And Main
In DTLA
I was blinded
By the sun
And He suddenly
Appeared
Riding an old yellow bicycle
while holding a black
Violin case in his left hand
A grin from ear to ear
Smothered his windburned
Face
I knew it was God
Because as he rode by
He made me
Inexplicably happy
And oh so briefly
Saul became Paul
And walked among
The Angels

Metro Stairs

Dingy Concrete Steps
In Pershing Square Station
One dirty Nike
Sneaker
Two steps from
The top
Without the benefit
Of Foot
Or leg attached
to a body.
A single
Shoe
Mute
Its Destination
Complete
Its Journey
Forever
A Mystery

AT
W A R B Y
P A R K E R

Downtown L.A.

Ensconced among

The Tattooed and Rainbow-Haired

The Gay and the Hip and the Ethnic

Wrapped in a Babel's Tower

Of Artistic Pretension

I am Surrounded by Rows of

Shape-shifting Chinese Frames

Round and Square and Large and Small

Multicolored Plastic With Snappy Preppy Names

That coo to the young

With promises of Intellect and Style

While they growl at me

Hating my Face and Mocking my Audacity

In Silvered Glass Reverse

I am a Thrift Store Suit

Dusty and Out of Style

Shaken and Put on Display

Among the Fresh and New
But I don't Care
Because I am Blind and In Need
Of Vision on the Cheap
I think it Ironic that Glasses
Have allowed me to Grow Old
Given me the Privilege to Witness
Each new crack in my Facade
Each Sunrise and Sunset
Each Travesty and Miracle
In Perfect False Convex Clarity
In another Age
I'd have fallen in a chasm
A Victim of Fauna with Teeth and Claws
Blurred Chimera Laughing at my Weakness
Cornea and Pupil Betraying Reality and Existence
A burden living in a Jacob-Deceiving-Isaac World
Poor Blind Boy Mocked by Mother Nature
Doomed to See Loved ones Clearly
Just Inches Away.
So I Try another Frame
And I Smile and I Cringe
Scringing I Decide
The Keeper of the Secret
That I may never
look good again
But At Least
I am still Alive

Girl on the Train

Her Hair was on Fire
Cascading down
Red and Yellow
Molten Lava
Against Cool White Skin
Flame Brushing
Glacial Eyes
Texting on Magenta Cell
She Briefly Touches Pink Leggings
with Stenciled Holes
Revealing Polka Dots
Of Alabaster Flesh
Fire and Ice
Blue duffel bag
Contrasting Hot Pink Top
She Looks up
Glimpsing Me
Glimpsing Her
I look away Embarrassed
Innocent and Fascinated

But to Her
I'm One of Many
Old Men
Staring and Leering
Wanting and Remembering
soft Flesh and Ecstatic Moans
I want to say No
I am not like the Others
You are a Work of Art
Your Hair A Flickering
Downdraft Candle Flame
Appreciation is not Erection
But I am not convinced
I am so different
Her cold sharp stare
Piercing Pretension
as I leave the train
at Pershing Square
Shamed by the Perceived Thought
of a Stranger on a Train

Rick Leddy

Too Too Many Many

Too Many Too Many Too Ma

I'm walking on the Boulevard of Too Many
Too Many Italian suits of specious provenance
Hanging wrinkled on browned manikins
Too Many skittle-colored suitcases
Crammed into hurricane-induced merchandising
Too Many plastic neon Jesus sculptures
And Mother Mary votives awaiting wax-fueled Pietà moments
Too Many people speaking in Babelous tongues
While those I comprehend talk only to themselves
Too Many shops smelling of leather and benzene
Blaring white-noise distorted mariachi trumpets
Too Many near-death flashing whiz-bang gizmos
Working on entropy an hour at a time
Too Many merchants with hollow eyes
Staring longingly at rushing humanity like winter-elk kill
Too Many shrink-wrapped sneakers
Guaranteed vacuum-sealed Nike freshness
Too Many things to take in
Sights and smells and sounds
That Rattle and Puree in my brain
Floating motes here and gone
I close my eyes against the barrage
Spirits of goods like ghosts dance grey against eyelids
Where do they all go, I wonder
These Too Many things
Where do they go?

Rick Leddy

Not Tonight

Rail of a greying black man
At Union Station
Says, Hey!
I say, I have no change
He cries indignant
You don't KNOW I was going to ask you that.
I want to say,
Were you going to ask me about my life?
Me, a stranger in a train station
We both know the score
I've been hit up for money in cathedrals, on street corners, in red
light districts, in bars, in restaurants, on trains, in train stations, in bus
stations, in airports, on the street, in my car, in hostels, in front of my
home, in parks, in snow, in freezing sleet, when I've been flush and when
I've been broke, in museums, in bars, in pubs, at school, in bathrooms,
with my wife, with my kids, when I was single, at morning, noon and
night, at breakfast, lunch and dinner, in nightclubs, at gas stations, in bad
and good neighborhoods, when I've been sick, when I've been ecstatic,
when I've been drunk, when I've been lonely, when I've felt like giving
and when I haven't, on every major holiday and all the days in between
And four times
By four different people
Tonight
Before you came up to me just now
So interested in my life
I have no money
So you attempt to take your pound of flesh in Guilt
But I'm not writing that check
For your dishonesty
Because I'm tapped
And I'm tired
And I won't stop
Not tonight

Rick Leddy

Glitter

Tripping over Batman
Black Zorro Complaining
Tourists snap memories
While Squatting on Stars
We Weave through
Confused and Distant Travelers
And Sidestep Hardened Humanity
Unimpressed by the Fabricated
Dirty Urban Lighthouse
Neon Screaming
HERE
is Where you Need To Be.
Hands and Feet
Locked In ambered concrete celebrity
call from Faux-Chinese Portico.
Joan Rivers in Wax
Front and Center
Beckons from the Newly Dead
Come Remember
When Glitter was Gold
On the Boulevard
a lifetime ago In Black and White.
Engulfed in the chaotic sea of
Winners and Losers
Gawkers and Dilettantes
Swimming in a Past and a Present
juxtaposed in Wishes and Reality
We leave behind
The Jumble
Of Manufactured Dreams

Hollywood/Vine

Rick Leddy

L.A. Haiku

Two brown shoes in lot
Sit side by side awaiting
Bad haiku treatment

Sleeping on the Metro
My lids
Open and close heavily
Darkness
And Then
Half Building
Tableaux From Window
Darkness
And Then
Pantomime Concert From
Cell Phone Rap Star.
Darkness
And Then
Onion-Head Gangster with
L.A. Ink on Neck
Darkness
And then

Monkey on a Dog

I'm a Monkey on a Dog
He said to me
Just Hanging on
But I don't know why
Waiting for rewards
I know won't come
Heaven's in a Glass
And Hell is when it's gone
I'm a Monkey on a Dog
Just Riding the Beast
Too Afraid To Fall
Because I might Fly
Going Round in Circles
Dressed With Nowhere to Go
Life's a rattle in my chest
That chills me to the bone
I'm a Monkey on a Dog
It's a one way ride
Grab hold of the fur
And watch for the teeth

ZOLTAR!

Zoltar Screamed / In My Peripheral Vision / From an Arcade

On 7th And Broadway / I Will Tell Your Fortune / Stop!

Leave Nothing to Chance! / I am Zoltar! / But I walked By Unconvinced

Him Being an Automaton And All / But Then I stopped

Visions of Tom Hanks / And Big flitting like 80s Fireflies In Mind's Eye

Could Zoltar be / A Harbinger / The Prophet / A Soothsayer of Old

Wrapped in Jiffy-Pop Turban / And Gibb Brothers Sleeves

Trapped Behind Clear Silicon / Inside a Carnival Arco station?

So, Turning Around / I returned to Zoltar, Mighty, Zoltar! / Space and Time

One And the Same / His Vision Long and Wisdom Deep

My Fate In His Plastic Hands / He held a Crystal Ball

That Glowed (of course) / One Dollar to learn my Fortune

A Bargain At Twice the Price / I Pledged my Gold

For Promise of Prescience / He moved Deliberately

Arm Sweeping from Right to Left / Mesmerizing Globe in Hand

His Lips not Moving / (he was that good) / Voice Booming and Projecting

Zoltar Speaks / What Do You Seek? / (A Rhetorical Question, I assumed)

I stared at the Tantalizing Slot / That read /

Fortune Teller Cards Tear Here / I awaited Release / To Know the Future

Frightened yet Exhilarated / I Waited / And Waited / And Waited

Was Zoltar Wise Beyond Wise? / Of Course / Existential Zoltar Knowing

The Future is Not to be Known / Our Paths Never Truly Divined

Or Etched in Stone / Otherwise we would Go Mad

A Message so Profound / And Sublime / That it was lost on me

As I shook Mighty Zoltar's abode / Demanding my money back

For a Fortune / That Would Never Come

Rick Leddy

Holographic Jesus

Walking Along 3rd
Between Los Angeles
And San Pedro
I saw a painting of
Holographic Jesus
Carrying A Cross
While Riding a Donkey
In a Mexican
Religious Art store
On the Same Block
As reflective shops
Selling Rows And Rows
Of Shiny Wholesale Bongs
Somehow it seemed
Appropriate that
Holographic Jesus
Carrying a Cross
While Riding a Donkey
Lived on this block
Biblical Inaccuracy
Aside

Metro Mona Lisa

Enigmatic Smile and
Symbiotic Lipstick
Fanned by Artificial Lashes
Yellow Homer Simpson Crop Top
Stereo Zirconium Earrings
Greet White iPhone earbuds
Unadulterated Joy Projected
She exits
At Highland Park Station
Smiling at A Secret
Only She Will
Ever Know

Pershing Square

Rick Leddy

Mirror
Mirror

Pretty young
Mexican girl
Talks to her mother
On the train
Not realizing
That she is
Speaking into
A mirror
Thirty Years in
The Future

Je T'aime

The thin white kid
Gets on the Gold Line
At the same time every day
From the Highland Park Station
He carries a long skateboard
With the Words
Death Wish
Scrawled in sketchy skateboard font
On the bottom of the deck
He looks anything but
A skateboarder cliche
Neatly cut hair
Conservative thin-cut brown pants
An aging steel grey down jacket
Osmond Concrete warrior
He sits beside me
Now, for the second or third time
I want to say
Long-time
But I know I won't
He dips his hand into a blue, green and yellow
Backpack
I think he will pull out a cell phone
Game Over
But he doesn't
He extricates a pocket book
That says Book of French Paraphrases
On the cover

He opens it and thumbs to the title

Romance

He concentrates intently on the book

Then raises his head slightly

His eyes closed

Repeating silently

A pocketbook phrase of love or endearment

Then back to the book

Again

And the cycle repeats

I wonder at the end of his journey

If a there is a girl

He is trying to impress

With soft whispered Gallic phrases

Or whether his plans are to visit

Paris

To find true romance

He exits at Union Station

I will probably see him again tomorrow

And I want to ask

Have you found true romance?

I want to say

I can remember being young and in love

But now I am old and in love

But it is different

But I won't

Because that is the way

Of the train

WELCOME TO THE
HISTORIC THEATRE
DISTRICT

A dog stops on
Broadway
To do his business
I stop
And stare.
Suddenly
I realize
That I will never
Be able to use
A self-serve
Frozen yogurt machine
Or Eat
Chocolate Frozen Yogurt
Again

Sick on the Red Line

I am ill today
Someone has filled my head
With toxic cotton balls
and is working an ice pick into
My right eye socket
Unrelentingly.
A man wearing a dark green Beanie yells,
"Yeah!" as he dances
In front of the open doors
of a Red Line train car
Another screams
WE ARE ALL GOING TO KILL OURSELVES
IT'S ONLY A MATTER OF TIME
BEFORE WE BLOW OURSELVES UP
as he strides past me, his voice red-shifting
Doom swallowed by the din of an arriving train.
And I think
Today
I should only be so
Lucky

ADD ADD ADD ADD

Mid-twenties, Mick Jagger doppelganger in a trucker cap
Testament To My Love tattooed down his white, thin forearm
Inked flames rising from the other
Counting twenties from his wallet
A yellow, crumpled Metro violation ticket falls out
He. Can't. Stop. Fidgeting.
Eyes glossed, movements slower than epilepsy
But Barely
He lives in Monrovia he tells a friend on the phone
The doctor says he should take the ADD medicine
But he thinks it doesn't work
He says as he runs his right hand
Up and down
Up and down
Up and down
His left arm

Samudaya Cell Phone

Buddhist Monk
Takes a call
on Samudaya cell phone
Hand to Ear
Suffering Having Many Causes
Including Dropped Calls
And Data Overages.
Digital Realization and
Unlimited Enlightenment Covered
In the Eightfold Monthly Plan
Nirvana Achieved
Through 4G LTE
Finding Peace and Truth
Upgrading Life and Devices
He disappears
Seeking wisdom
And Strong Connection
Through the Five Bar Path

Hallelujah Honkey

Black Church Lady
Ambles on the train
Supported by Aluminum
Extra-skeleton With Wheels
Dressed in Purple
Like Southern Baptist Royalty
A Floppy Straw Hat
Ringed With Forest Green Vegetation
Relaxes on her head
I want to Say
Amen Sister
You are beautiful
God Surely Smiles
On you and your
mixed Blue and Red Demeanor
and Your Rain Forest Chapeau
I want to Sing and Sway
And Let the Lord through the Door
Opened up by Organ and Bass
Hymnal riffs belted to the heavens
A sacrifice in notes lifted to the JC
Punctuated by rhythmic clapping
As peals of Thunder
shake the Pearly Gates
But it is your stop
And I am White
And was raised German Lutheran
And we don't do those things

SHIT

Happens
Happens

He sits silently on the Gold Line train
A leather jacket precariously held together
with Dirt and Despair,
Its fashion expiration date
like urban curdled Milk.
His spattered brown Chuck Taylor high-tops
Accidental and out of context
The wrong life attached
to hipster retro footwear
His eyes a memory
Behind mirrored sun glasses
A baseball cap reading
In thick brown letters:
Shit Happens
rests on his bobbing head
Like a thought balloon
stating the obvious

Rick Leddy

At the
Downtown
Garment Sale

Bony Westside Women
Jeans precisely torn
Gym memberships tattooed
on boyish hips
Parade past me
Style a prerequisite
Not a choice
But I don't care
Because all I want is
Coffee

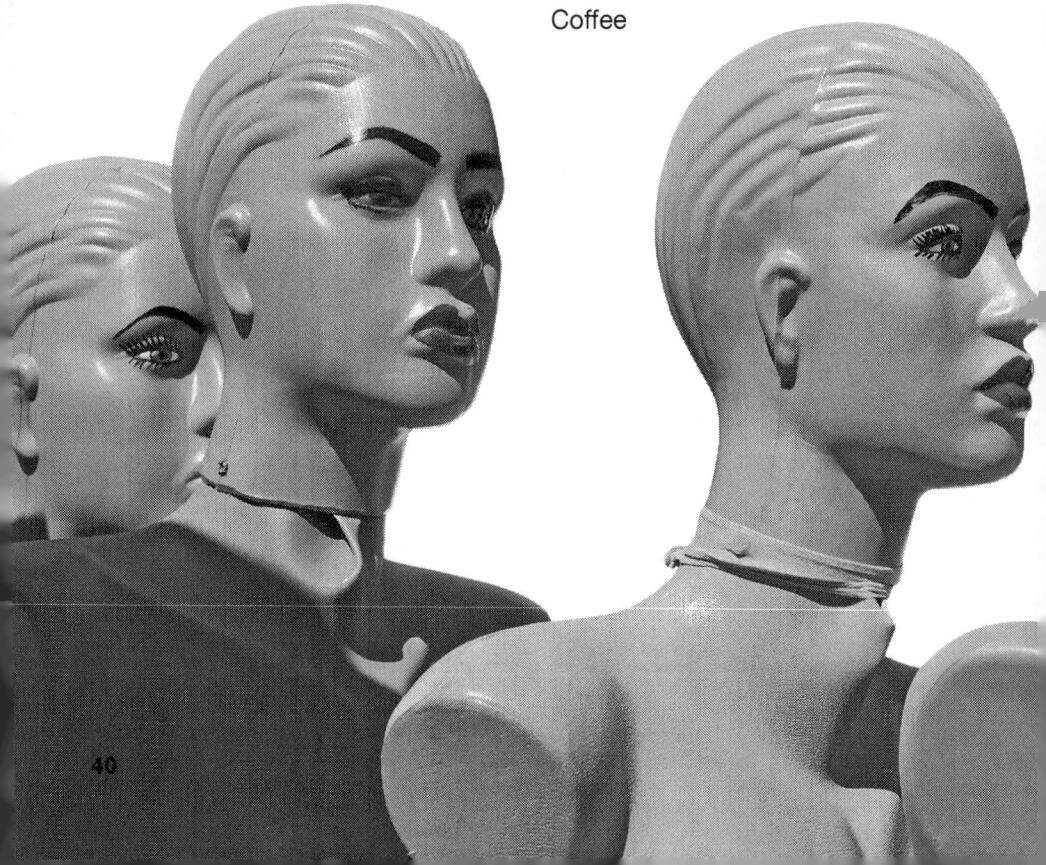

Last Year's Model

At Scalpel's Edge
Glinting razor-sharp salvation
Paralyzing pin-pricks to soothe
the ravages of time
Fear of replacement
By next year's model
drove her to
fight Nature and God
Her Hands of Time
blue-veined and spotted
translucent Skin
A Mocking Mirror Transparently Reflecting
the Truth as she Sees it
A Fresh Coat of Paint
on thickening layers
Betting on Beauty
when the House always Wins
She walks Triumphant
in the Valley of the Shadow
As Younger versions of herself
Fresh, Bold and Everywhere
Eye her casually
Unaware they are staring at the Future
As she strides into the Past

Black Hair
Black Leather Jacket
Black Skirt
Black Tights
And Black Shoes
Accented by a shock
Of Ruby Red Lips
Stuffs her small dog
Into a brown knapsack

Blue Dinosaur

And throws them both
Onto her back
Reverse Kangaroo
His brown head
Pops out of the opening
Of the worn pouch
A Synchronicity
Giving the appearance
Of an exotic Duffel Creature
Only
The dog is wearing
A blue garment
With a hoodie attached
That is a
Dinosaur Head.

She gets on the train
Removes the knapsack
And puts it on her lap.
The dog
Still in the knapsack
Falls asleep against her chest
Perhaps Dreaming of
Chasing birds in his
Blue Dinosaur Hoodie

Hoodie

30 Years Younger

She sat next to me at Hollywood Bowl
Star tattoos on smooth white knees
Black Ink decorating long, delicate fingers
Short hair the color of moonless night
tucked beneath black beanie
Young and fresh and bright
Smelling of future and potential
Striding unafraid into the New World
with meticulous hipster cred.
I gave her furtive glances
Thinking If I was only 30 years younger…
Once I could lie to myself convincingly
But Honesty is the self-inflicted
curse of experience

Lies once thick and opaque
have become brittle yellowed pieces
of cellophane that crumble
and fly in barely breeze
And I knew
If I was 30 years younger
My words would still be trapped
In black hole throat
caught forever in a swirling
event horizon of doubt
Random crossed and
opportune paths
Vanishing for lack of utterance;
If I was 30 years younger

nothing would have changed.
She a specter in peripheral vision
Sitting next to a mute
made of dark matter
afraid to embrace the lovely chaos.
Experience murdered of its potential
by silence and fear of rejection.
Instead choosing to Walk
down the safe, straight road
And always wondering
What if?
If I was 30 years younger
Is always the domain of
Old and foolish men.

Metro Picasso

A young, round woman
With sad eyes and dark features
is drawing.
There is a Pee Wee Herman button
Affixed to her denim jacket.
A sad girl holding a bag
Slowly emerges on a page
of her small spiral bound notebook.
She uses ball-point pens
But somehow makes the lines
Delicate
She looks out the window
of the moving Gold Line Train
Thinking

Then carefully places a circle
in the perfect spot.
It is a nice drawing
Of a lonely girl
Standing in front of an
Ink black sky.
And I wonder if it is her
in the drawing.
She closes the book
And gently places it into
Her worn brown messenger bag
And gets out at Highland Park
And I will never know
If she is the girl in the drawing.

Pigment
Conundrum

She stared vacantly
Out of the moving train window
A tattoo of an ornate Victrola
with a hummingbird feeding from it
etched on her arm.
And I Thought
Sometimes
Ink
Just
Baffles
Me

The Walk

Between 8th and 1st on Broadway
Barista with Half-Shaved Head
Paints Artful Latte
Humming Blurred Lines chorus
His Repeated Musical Rosary;
Thin Man On Sidewalk Wades in Concrete
His Leg Stumps Stuffed
In Silver Tote Bag;
Compro Oro Shouts in Red and Gold
Fronted by Bored Uniforms Dreaming of
Gangsters and Burritos;
Hipster sitting on a chair
Half-Eaten Popsicle in Hand
Being photographed next to

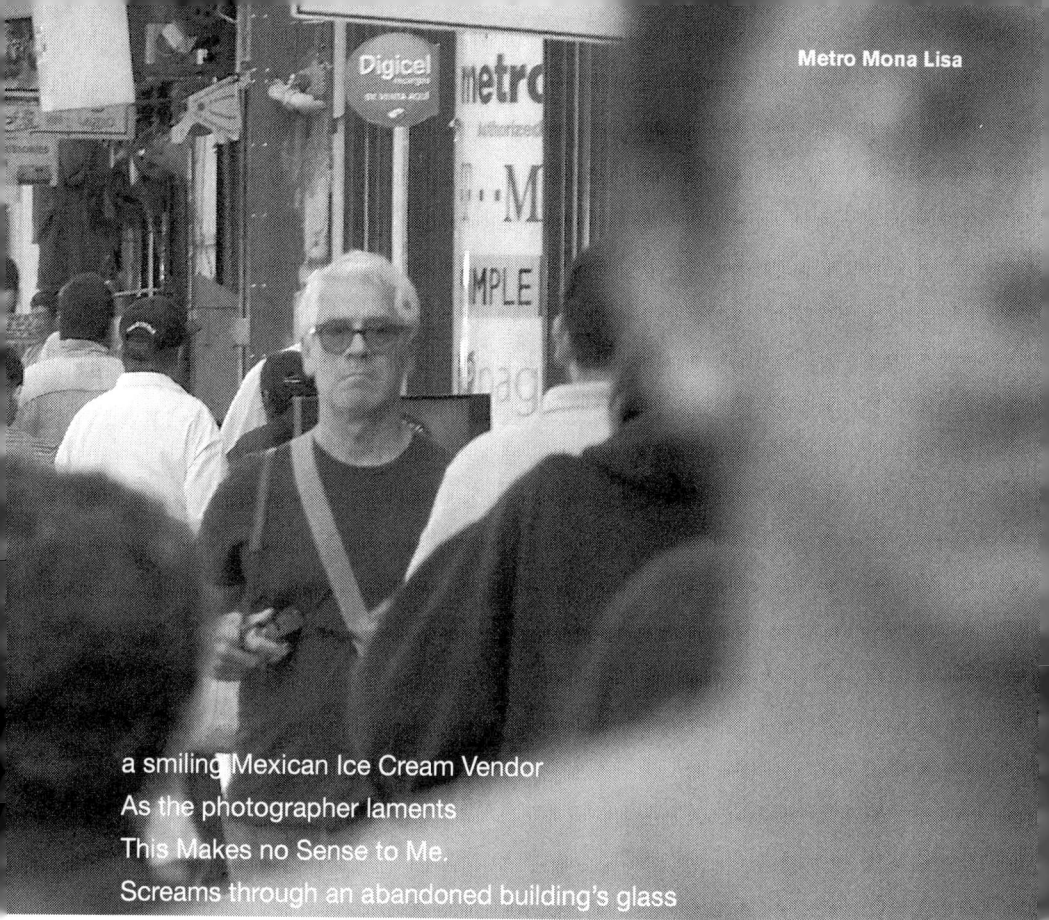

a smiling Mexican Ice Cream Vendor
As the photographer laments
This Makes no Sense to Me.
Screams through an abandoned building's glass
as Black male model decked in Reflective Silver Stripes
descends stairs with neon models clinging
All affecting False Fashionista Joy
while staccato metered light silently explodes;
Dirt smudged Black Pippi Longstocking
Braids Sticking Out Like Disheveled Wings
A Homeless Aircraft With
Nowhere to Land;
A small Chinese woman hands out garish fliers
that state, Dios Te Ama
(English Version Next Page)
God Loves You
(Version en espanol reverso);
And today, at least
I believe that is True

Perfect Ten

Perfect Ken
Got on the Train
His Hair
Immutable Helmeted Perfection
His White Dress Shirt
As Straight and Unwrinkled
As Virginal Movie Screen
Black Bag in Hand
Sporting Unpronounceable Logo
Women Whip-lashed
By His Stray Pheromones
He bores a hole
In iPhone Screen
Cerulean Eyes Sparkling
Smiling Piano-Keyed
White and Smooth
I am Hating
Perfect Ken
For a Myriad of Sins
Not His Own
When
He grabs His Board-Straight Tie
And Wipes His Nose
With It
The Universe Pauses
Winks
And Is in Balance
Once Again

Carpe...

Tonight was going to be the Night
When I seized a free sample
Of bite-sized chunks of Wetzel's Pretzels
that are handed out at Union Station
Before the entrance to the Red Line.
I had passed up the free treats
a dozen times before
But Tonight, was the Night
When I was going to throw caution
To the Wind

And grab the offering
And gobble it down
As if I had never eaten before
My mouth was watering
My heart racing just a bit faster
In anticipation
But, The Wetzel girl
Wasn't there
And all I could think was
Carpe Pretzel

Line of school children
At Chinatown Station
Walk in line
A Cacophony of
Anticipatory Field Trip Chatter
Man in brown jacket
Carrying plastic shopping bag
Enters the train
Pivots on heel
At the open door
And waves
Saying,
Jesus loves the little children
Go with love children
The doors close
And then
All is
Silent
Again

Rick Leddy

Another Day in Gotham West

Batman was walking
On the platform
At Union Station
Today
His mask
hiked on his forehead
revealing eyes
rounded with
black makeup.
A crime fighting
Raccoon.
He looked
Older and
More Depressed
And More Mexican
In real life.
Perhaps the Batmobile
Had broken down
And he needed to take the
Red Line.
Nobody gave him a
Second Look.
Just another
Super Hero
Going home
After a hard day
At the office

Mr. Many Pens

At the Highland And Hollywood
Red Line Station
Mr. Many Pens
Awaits the Train
Six shiny pens clipped
Dutifully To His pale yellow
Shirt pocket
Soldiers aligned in defense
against the Unsigned Document
or the Un-Notarized Note
Waging war on the Digital Age
His weapons at ready
An Anachronism in Ball Point
Steely-eyed Defender of Ink
Hoarding Sleek Missiles of Literacy
His Loins Girded
At ready for the proffered Checkbook
Armed for the Battle of the Book Signing
Mr. Many Pens is Prepared
For the Coming Analog Storm
That is sure to come

Rick Leddy

Half a Man

Silent Movie / I stuff my earphones / Into my ears
Before I get on the train / And amputate
my experience of the World.
Podcast mysteries of butterfly chrysalis / Are learned /
but nothing of Humanity.
The train has become a Marcel Marceau Tableaux
A girl with severe orange and black eye makeup
Speaks intently with her boyfriend;
a silent movie with no context.
I am not the only cripple on the train / Most have
earphones stuffed into ears / Hidden behind walls
of private sound / Barricaded against / fellow travelers
Seeing, but not comprehending
Nor attempting / to participate
or feign Interest in the Wonder of it all.
I get off the train / At Pershing Square
A man asks me a question/
I cannot hear him / And I move on
Without stopping /
Because my earphones have made others
Invisible /
And have left me
Half/ a/ Man

My earbuds are like
Past Relationships
Some were comfortable
While others hurt.
I believed in some
But the fit was incomplete.
Some broke down with no explanation
Leaving me confused and frustrated.
While others were unlistenable
Filling my head with incomprehensible static.
I have fallen for the pretty ones
Full of allure and promise
But found them shallow and lacking.
I have fond memories of some
And miss them.
While others were throwaways
Used without much thought.
Others simply disappeared
Without a trace
Leaving thin hope they
would return someday
But knowing deep down
They were gone forever
I tried to give up and
Swear off audio salvation
Uttering bitter recriminations
Of ever finding
The Right Ones
Only to be lured back
By promises that
This time it will be different
Then Falling
For those sweet lies
Again
And
Again
And

**AURAL
Sex**

You Were Here

The Googlemobile
At Alameda and Second
Jetson Green Camera on Wheels
Snowden Sedan
Automated Minion driven in quest
for World Domination
It glides by Silent as a Shark
that has swallowed an immigrant
Has it caught my image
Captured my soul
Will I be forever
Trapped in
Digital Street-View Purgatory
Zoomed into
An Accidental Actor
In an Accidental Scene
For an Accidental Tourist
A Time Traveler
Locked in the Past
In Ones and Zeros
Strangers not caring
About my life and loves and fears
Just Walking Urban Wallpaper
Decorating a Destination?
I walk to the Train
Strangely hoping
That Google Dreamcatcher
Has Snapped my Existence
If for nothing else
To prove I was here
And had scratched the surface
Of the World
Ever so slightly and briefly

WhIstle Woman

Whistle Woman on 4th
Blows her whistle
An NFL game every 10 Feet
Homeless Referee
Pacing off perceived penalties
Infractions clear in her own mind
The city in illegal motion
Her life flagged for unnecessary roughness
Shrilly blowing perceived fouls
As she paces to a goal
In a game where nobody
Is keeping score

Accidental Jesus
Trades water for wine
Gave it all up
To fight demons full time
Forsaken by Father
Hung dry on the cross
He screams to the heavens
For miracles lost
The sins that he died for
Were sins of his own
Forgiveness forgotten
In dark alleys alone
Hope is a gospel
Words for the deaf
Light flickering to shadows
In the valley of death

Accidental JeSuS

Rick Leddy

Metro Ink

I sit in back of
Gold Line Illustrated Man
A Photo-Realistic Tattoo
Scarface Steely-eyed Above
flannel shirt collar
Say Hello to My Little Friend
Taunting me
From the Back of his head
Illustrated Man
Puts on a backward cap
LA written in
Silk-screened open Safety Pins
Scarface Disappears
Beneath Battered Brown Bill
Illustrated Man
Turns Slightly
To Commune with Cell
His face a Swirl of
Tantalizing Colors
A Barber Shop Pole
Or is it Venice with Stars
I cannot tell
A diamond stud above his eye
AMER begins at his right temple
I fill in the blanks
ICA imagined retort on forehead
I can't be sure
Thirsting to Know
An itch not scratched
I want to study you

An art opening of living
Flesh and Color
Face Covered in Abstraction
Body Revealing Nothing
Wanting X-ray Specs
To Unleash Unseen Canvas
Hidden Beneath your Clothes
Mission Station comes
I Purposely Pick an Escape
Not my own
I face him
And see James Dean
Or is it Christopher Walken
Staring at me from
His open shirt
My personal Illustrated Man
A Black Handlebar Mustache
Floating on Kaleidoscope Visage
He has gone All In
A Path Paved On Epidermis
I leave and walk
To La Monarca Bakery
And wait in line behind
Hipster wearing Vans and
Thick black-rimmed glasses
A Skull and Chinese Letters inked
on his Bicep
Easily hidden with proper cloth
And I can't help but think
Uncommitted Poseur

Young Dog

Old Dog

In Highland Park, the young Hispanic man gets on the train heading downtown. He is all serious and hard with his un-tucked button down shirt, baggy pants and baseball cap with the bill straight as a runway. He sits next to me and is looking out the window. Suddenly, his head jerks up and he sits up tightly, giving something his rapt attention. He is all concentration. Curious, I follow his laser stare. He is looking at a petite young woman walking down the platform. The train moves and he relaxes back into cool indifference. Next stop, Southwest Museum Station, he bolts to attention again. This time it's a larger young Hispanic woman carrying a tricycle that has caught his attention. The doors close, the train moves and he assumes his familiar cool, hard position. I'm old, but I'm not dead. I get it. But, I can't help thinking that he is acting exactly like my dog when he sees a squirrel. There is the sudden snap to attention. The rapt concentration as he follows his prey. Tense. Focused. There is only the squirrel in the circle at the end of his tunnel vision. It makes me want to yell, "Down, boy!" And suddenly, I have the realization that men really are dogs — especially young men. I remember when it was like that. When the suggestion of flowing hair in my peripheral vision or the hint of perfume in the summer air caused me to stop, stare hard and wonder, "Do I leap? Do I chase?" He gets off the train at the Lincoln/ Cypress Park Station — and the old dog follows the path of the young pup as he walks down the platform while the train moves slowly and we head in opposite directions.

Rick Leddy

God is

ONE WAY

66

in the Lights

Now And Then
I Throw Caution to The Wind
And let Traffic Signals
Determine My Fate
Walking With
Path in Mind
Breeds Contempt
For Random Experience
GPS Meaning
Great Potential Sapping
Rejection of Orbital Bytes
Determining My Path
Sometimes I follow Green
Where it takes me
A Zig Past Barking Dog
A Zag Past lit windows
Tableaux of Lives I will never know
Crossing With Bright Walking Man
Before the Countdown Begins
Illuminated Virgil
My Guide
Through a Paradise Found —
Past the
Straight and Narrow
And Into
The Wondrous and Unknown

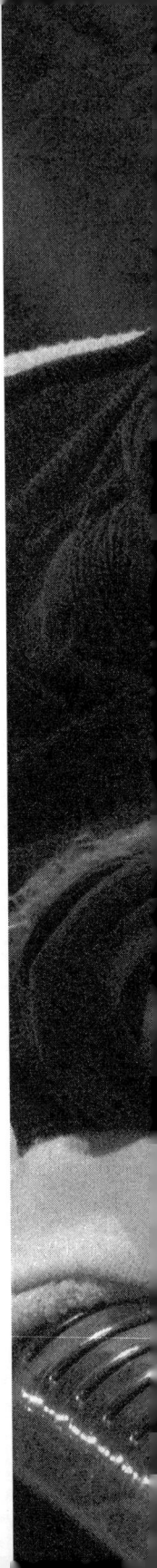

What
Dreams...

What dreams can be dreamt
When supported by hard-slatted metal
And open air
Our judgment as harsh as the unfiltered sun
Invisible to light and vision
She escapes from the exhaustion
Of existence
A vocabulary stunted
Hope ripped from her pages
She sleeps as the child she was
And we walk by
Quietly
Fearful of waking
The nightmare
Inside us

Rick Leddy

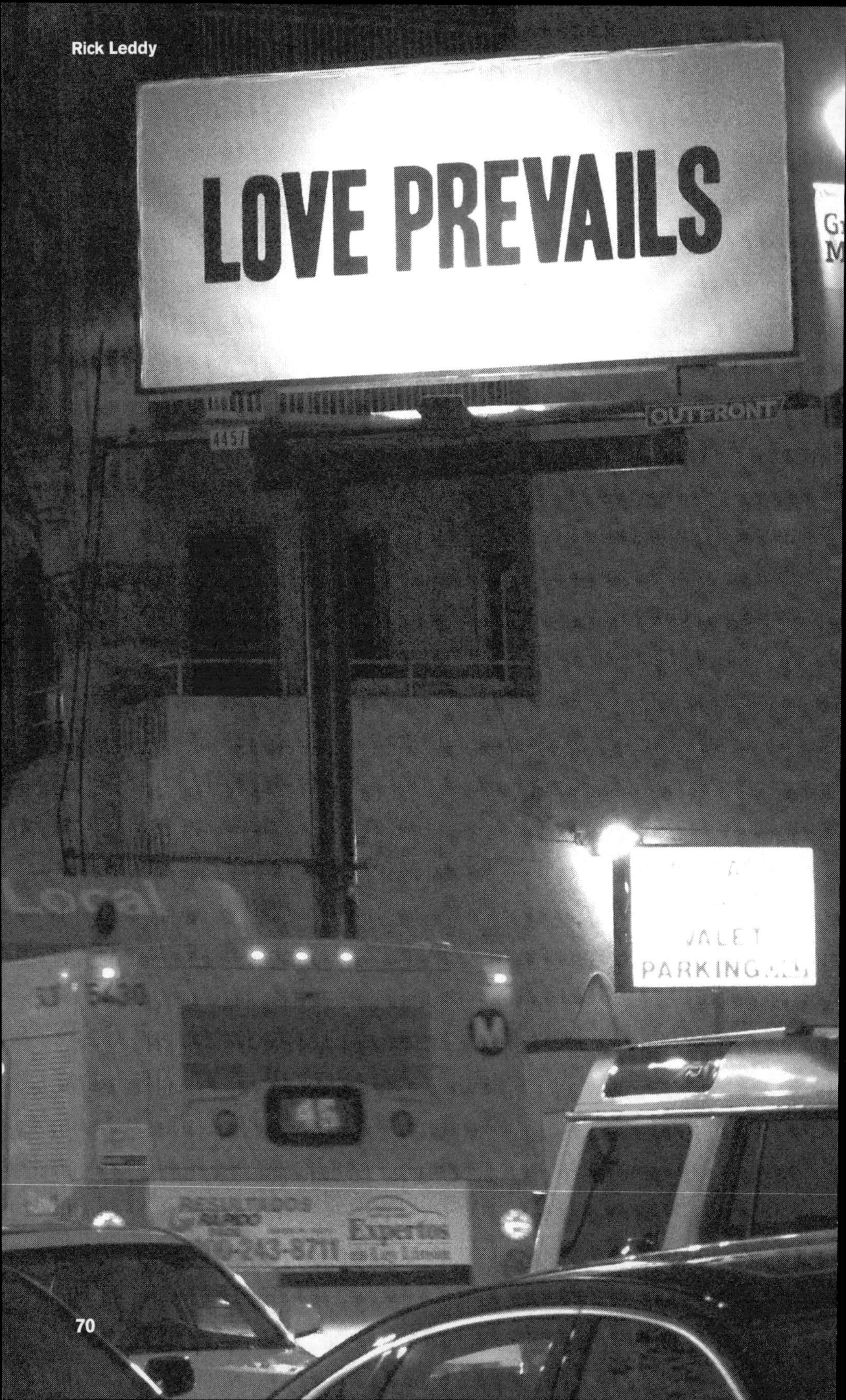

The city screams
smoke and desperation
Drought-laden concrete sizzles
hard and hot under unmerciful skies
white with anger and promise
Shadows move within shadows
while hidden refugees pray
in converted theatre churches
that Love Prevails
Wind-burned and sun-stroked lives
A Babel-tower of languages
speaking volumes in cacophonous mix
Vendors beckon beside the mountainous and chaotic
weight of the American Dream
as Mothers hide beneath ornate
and rusted matinee idol overhangs
their children impossibly asleep in strollers amid
the perpetual pounding urban Sturm and Drang
Genuflecting against banshees of violence and poverty
and crying to the heavens
That Love Prevails
Walking among the hip and hopeless
My vision burned and blurred
by the searing stream of passing lives
Buildings rise and crumble
Living, dying and resurrected memories unfold
The city of a million hopes and stillborn dreams
Laid before me
My mouth dry, my lips cracked
as Valkyries swarm the desert stolen city sky
My heart howls and my blood-filled ears pound
As I implore to the echoing madness and beauty
Let Love Prevail

Parece Que No Estamos en Kansas Más

At night

In Highland Park

There is a shining beacon

It glows like a magical moving city

Oz melting angry witches of hunger

The Gold Line Road leading

To Gringo Dorito-infused Chalupa

And I know I must find it

Because sometimes all we need

Is a goal in life

And Mine

Right now

Is a Seven-Layer Burrito

Rick Leddy

Le Lune de Soleil

She wears a white T-shirt
With A Black and White Print
That Says Le Lune
On the front.
Only the graphic moon
Has a halo of flames
And in the Center
Is a pyramid with an eye.
I ponder the mystery of a
Flaming Moon with
Masonic Overtones.
She is Young and all Concentration
Doing needlepoint.
The hoop Neon Orange
Surrounds an Unseen Design
Forming With each stab and pull of
the Needle.
Suddenly
The needle unthreads.
Undaunted and Expertly

She threads it
Even as the train jostles
And mocks her efforts.
We reach Union Station
And she places the needlepoint
In her Backpack
Stands
And her T-shirt
Reveals Le Soleil
Inscribed on the bottom
Explaining
The Flaming Moon.
One Mystery solved
But another in place
That will be shrouded forever —
The blank canvas
Of the needlepoint design
I will never be able
To Fill

Purgatory Found

In the span of an Hour

I've converted to Catholicism

Because I have Discovered

Purgatory

In a Downtown

Jury Assembly Room

This
ain't
Disneyland
Mutha
F**ka

Angry Bus Stop Woman screams
To syncopated metal crashing against asphalt
A blurred green arm wielding a shiny rod
Beating Psychotic Morse Code
Pure vitriol directed at the
horizontal cracked and hostile pavement
Her voice spits gravel
at Imaginary enemies
spewing grave injustice
as I redshift down the sidewalk
outpacing the hate-filled Sirocco
Walking in the valley of the shadow
of Main Street USA
On the border of
her involuntary Fantasyland

Then I turned / And the slatted metal window neon / Screamed that
Life must be lived / Because it is all we really know / Heaven is faith /
And Hell is what we say we will do tomorrow and know we won't /
Waiting for an afterlife / Instead of loving life
This one
Now
Today

Rick Leddy

ART ART ART ART

WalkWalkWalkWalk

A chaotic salad of humanity
Mixed with smells of patchouli, Incense
and biological stew
Young woman in impossible pantsuit
Gyrates with lighted hoop
beside an exuberant B movie alien partner
Aging Hari Krishna with Barbie Doll cymbals
Sings to fashionista dogs
Duo with banjo and harp play
resonate notes piercing the cacophony
of a thousand lives rushing
from here to there
Salmon swimming upstream
against an undulating river of flesh and blood
Artist dressed as hipster nymph
Sits painting hands on wood
Glowing legs and high cheekbones
more statement than her art
Humanity more the show than
attention screaming ideas on walls
As the night swallows perception whole
And the block becomes a prowling creature
Preying on senses and hunting for difference
Youth stalking experience while
sweating pheromones into the restless night
Grasping each moment and squeezing
the light until it runs dry

Special acknowledgments:

I would like to thank Mosh Levin for use of his photo of Zoltar (p. 25). When I went back to photograph Zoltar, Mighty, Zoltar on Broadway, the arcade had shuttered permanently. Luckily, Mosh had a photo of another Zoltar (or is it the same one? Cue eerie music).

Also, great thanks goes to Erin Behl at PetitDogApparel who let me use her dog photo for my poem "Blue Dinosaur Hoodie" (pp. 42-43). Check out her amazing items on Etsy.

I would also like to thank my wife, Vanora, who offered constructive and intelligent criticism during this endeavor. Amazingly, I actually listened to some of it and the book is the better for it.

Also, I owe Gina Phelps a huge debt of gratitude. She found a laughable number of typos I had missed, including a spelling error of the word "editor" below, which was both horrifying and hysterically ironic.

Lastly, If not for the support of friends in life and on Facebook, Metro Mona Lisa would have remained a mind mirage — a chimera lost in the everyday — and little else. Thank you for encouraging and believing.

About the Author:

Rick Leddy is an author, cartoonist, art director, editor and poet who grew up in Los Angeles and continues to call it home. You will find him fending off imaginary enemies in the park when he isn't writing or drawing.

Made in the USA
San Bernardino, CA
07 September 2015